Take off Track and Field

SPORTS STARTERS

Robin Johnson

Crabtree Publishing Company

www.crabtreebooks.com

SPORTS STARTERS

Created by Bobbie Kalman

Author
Robin Johnson

Project coordinator
Kathy Middleton

Editor
Lynn Peppas

Photo research
Crystal Sikkens

**Production coordinator
and prepress technician**
Katherine Berti

Design
Katherine Berti

Print coordinator
Katherine Berti

Photographs
Keystone Press: ZUMAPRESS.com: pages 24, 28;
  Randy Pench/ZUMA: page 29
Shutterstock: front cover, pages 1, 5 (top), 6–7,
  7 (right), 17, 21, 22, 23; Natursports: back cover,
  pages 4 (left), 9, 16; David Boston: page 3; Denis
  Kuvaev: pages 4–5, 5 (bottom right), 10, 15, 18,
  30; IgorKa: page 8; Maxisport: pages 11, 14;
  Hasan Shaheed: page 12; Jerry Zitterman: page 13;
  Diego Barbieri: pages 19, 20; thelefty: page 25;
  Ververidis Vasilis: page 26; Aspen Photo: page 27
Wikimedia Commons: U.S. Navy photo by Gary
  Nichols: page 31

Library and Archives Canada Cataloguing in Publication

CIP available at Library and Archives Canada

Library of Congress Cataloging-in-Publication Data

Johnson, Robin (Robin R.)
 Take off track and field / Robin Johnson.
   p. cm. -- (Sports starters)
 Includes Index.
 ISBN 978-0-7787-3154-2 (reinforced library binding : alk. paper) -- ISBN
 978-0-7787-3181-8 (pbk. : alk. paper) -- ISBN 978-1-4271-9062-8 (electronic
 pdf) -- ISBN 978-1-4271-9116-8 (electronic html)
 1. Track and field--Juvenile literature. I. Title.

 GV1060.55.J64 2013
 796.42--dc23

                                        2012035163

Crabtree Publishing Company

Printed in Canada/102012/MA20120817

www.crabtreebooks.com   1-800-387-7650
Copyright © **2013 CRABTREE PUBLISHING COMPANY**. All rights reserved. No part of this publication may be reproduced, stored in a retrieval
system or be transmitted in any form or by any means, electronic, mechanical, photocopying, recording, or otherwise, without the prior written permission
of Crabtree Publishing Company. In Canada: We acknowledge the financial support of the Government of Canada through the Canada Book Fund for our
publishing activities.

Published in Canada
Crabtree Publishing
616 Welland Ave.
St. Catharines, Ontario
L2M 5V6

Published in the United States
Crabtree Publishing
PMB 59051
350 Fifth Avenue, 59th Floor
New York, New York 10118

Published in the United Kingdom
Crabtree Publishing
Maritime House
Basin Road North, Hove
BN41 1WR

Published in Australia
Crabtree Publishing
3 Charles Street
Coburg North
VIC 3058

Contents

Run, jump, and throw

Track and field is a sport made up of many different events. Events in track and field involve running, jumping, or throwing, or a combination of each. In running events, the **competitor** with the fastest time wins the race. In jumping events, the person who jumps the farthest or highest wins. In throwing events, the competitor who throws an object the farthest gets the gold.

Long jump competition

3000-meter race

Head to head

In most track and field events, individual athletes compete against each other. Jumpers and throwers take turns competing in field events. Runners race beside each other in track events. Some track events are **relay** races. In relays, each member of a team completes part of the race then passes a baton, or tube, to the next runner.

javelin competition

5

Field of dreams

Track and field competitions are held outdoors or in **stadiums**. Jumping and throwing events take place on large, flat fields. The fields are covered with real grass or fake grass called turf. Running races are held on long, oval tracks that surround the fields.

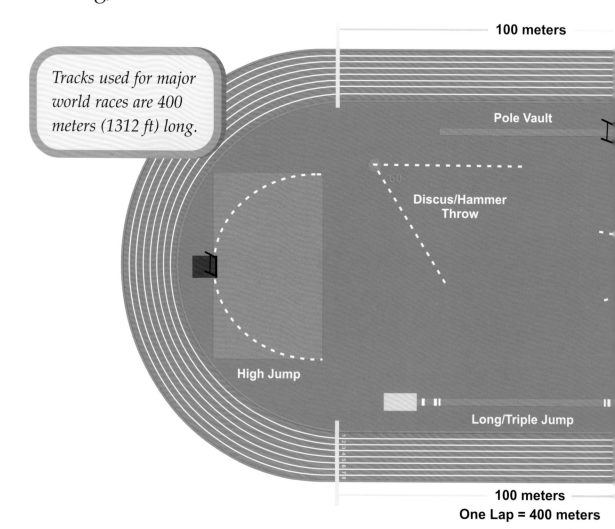

Tracks used for major world races are 400 meters (1312 ft) long.

100 meters

Pole Vault

Discus/Hammer Throw

High Jump

Long/Triple Jump

100 meters

One Lap = 400 meters

Fast track

Competition tracks are made of special rubber and other materials. Racers can run faster on these springy tracks than on other surfaces. Running tracks are divided into narrow sections called **lanes**. Most tracks have six to eight lanes. The track races are measured in metric units because most countries around the world use the metric system for measuring.

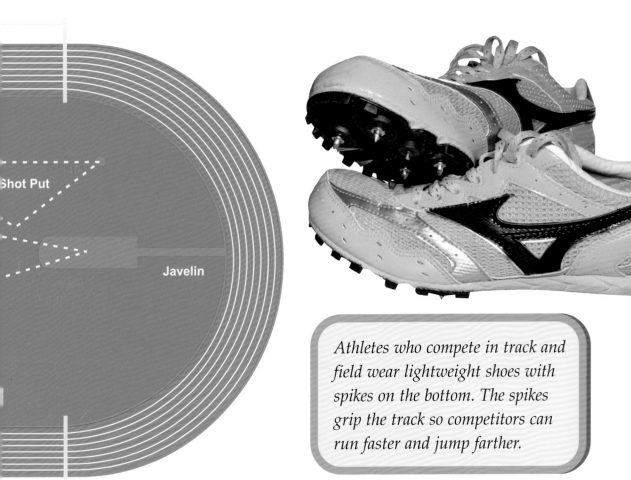

Shot Put

Javelin

Athletes who compete in track and field wear lightweight shoes with spikes on the bottom. The spikes grip the track so competitors can run faster and jump farther.

Race to the finish

*This race has a staggered start. The runners put their feet in **starting blocks**. They push off from the blocks to get a fast start.*

For short races, every runner begins at the same starting line. For races around the entire track, the starting lines are **staggered**. The outer lanes of an oval track are longer than the inner lanes. To make the distance of each lane the same for each runner, the starting line in each lane must be farther along the track than the lane to its left. A whistle or a shot from a starting gun begins the race. If someone starts to run before the whistle blows, it is called a false start. All the runners must return to the starting line and begin the race again.

This electronic timer shows minutes, seconds, and tenths of a second. Some even show to the nearest hundredth of a second!

Every second counts

Referees use electronic timers or stopwatches to time the races. Race times are measured in minutes and seconds. The first person to cross the finish line wins the race. A runner's entire **torso** must cross the line, not just their arms, legs, or head.

On track

Running races can be short, middle, or long distances. All races are measured in meters. Short races are 100 meters (328 ft), 200 meters (656 ft), or 400 meters (1312 ft) in length. These short races are called **sprints**.

In sprints, competitors run as hard and fast as they can for the entire race.

Go the distance

Middle-distance races are 800 meters (2625 ft), 1500 meters (4921 ft), or 3000 meters (9843 ft) long. Long-distance races are 5000 or 10,000 meters (16,404 or 32,808 ft) in length. Runners must try not to tire themselves out too soon in long races.

*Runners competing in middle- and long-distance races, like this 5000-meter race, must have a lot of **stamina** in order to finish the race.*

Relay races

In relay races, teams of four runners compete against one another. Each team member takes a turn running one **leg,** or section of the race. In the 4x100-meter race, each runner sprints for 100 meters (328 ft). In the longer 4x400-meter race, each team member runs 400 meters (1312 ft).

The final runner on a relay team is called the anchor.

Passing the baton

Runners in relay races carry batons. Batons are light, hollow tubes. When a runner finishes his or her leg, the runner passes the baton to the next member of the team. The baton is passed from one runner to the next. The final member of a relay team carries the baton across the finish line.

*Runners are usually **disqualified** if they drop the baton or, in the 4x100-meter race, touch the line of their lane.*

Jumping hurdles

In some track races, people must jump over obstacles called hurdles. Hurdles are high, lightweight bars that are spaced evenly along a track. Racers try to run and jump over the bars without losing speed.

Hurdles are used only in short-distance races.

In the clear

To **clear** a hurdle, a runner sprints toward it at top speed. The runner lifts his or her first leg, or **lead leg**, up and over the hurdle. Then the second leg, or **trail leg**, is lifted sideways over the hurdle. If the runner does not clear the obstacle, the hurdle will fall to the ground.

There is no penalty for hitting or knocking over hurdles in a race. However, it does slow the runner down.

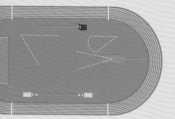

Raising the bar

The pole vault and high jump also involve clearing obstacles. In these field events, competitors try to leap over high bars without knocking them down. After jumpers have cleared the bar at one level, it is raised higher in the air. If a competitor knocks down the bar three times in a row, he or she is **eliminated** from the event.

The person who clears the highest bar wins the competition.

Flying high

In the high jump, people run and throw their bodies up and over a bar. High jumpers use only their speed and strength to lift themselves into the air. In the pole vault, people use long, bendy poles to launch themselves over a very high bar. The best competitors in the world can soar more than 6 meters (20 ft) in the air!

A pole vaulter sprints down a runway, then plants their pole in a box in the ground. They use the pole to launch themselves over the bar.

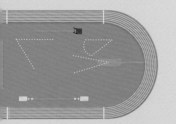

Jump for joy

The long jump and triple jump are distance-jumping events. In the long jump, competitors sprint down a track, then jump forward into a sandpit. The jumps are measured from a **foul line**, or takeoff mark, at the end of the track to the nearest mark in the sand made by the jumper. Jumps do not count if a competitor's feet go past the foul line.

Each competitor gets three jumps. The person with the longest jump wins the long jump event.

Hop, step, and jump

In the triple jump, athletes run at top speed down a track until they reach a takeoff mark on the track. Then they take one hop with one leg, take a long step with the other leg, and then jump into the sandpit on both feet. The length of the jump is measured from the takeoff mark on the track to the closest mark in the sand. Each competitor gets three tries to land the best jump. The person who hops, steps, and jumps the farthest wins.

The takeoff mark shown here is a red line on the runway with two pieces of striped wood on either side.

Throw it down

There are four throwing events in track and field. In the javelin throw, competitors toss a long, light spear as far as they can. Competitors hold the javelin with one hand and sprint down a runway. When they reach the end of the runway, they throw the javelin forward over their shoulder. The competitor with the farthest throw wins.

Competitors need speed and strength to win the javelin throw.

Heavy metals

The shot put, discus throw, and hammer throw are all strength events. To begin each event, throwers take their place inside a circle marked on the field. The throwers spin around and then hurl a heavy shot, discus, or hammer as far as possible. Competitors each get three throws. The farthest throw wins the event.

A shot is a heavy metal ball.

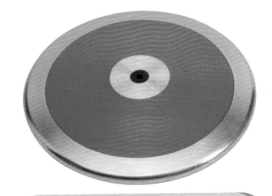

A discus is a heavy round disk.

A hammer is a heavy steel ball on a long wire.

Combined events

Combined events include both track races and field events. Pentathlons are made up of five different events. The events are the high jump, long jump, shot put, hurdles, and 800-meter race. Heptathlons have seven different events, and decathlons have ten events.

Pentathlon	*high jump*	*long jump*	*shot put*	*hurdles*
Heptathlon	*high jump*	*long jump*	*shot put*	*hurdles*
Decathlon	*high jump*	*long jump*	*shot put*	*hurdles*

Best all around

Combined events usually take place over two days. Competitors earn points for each event. The person with the highest total score wins the competition. To win combined events, people must be good all-around athletes.

1500m (men) 800m (women)					
60m (men) 200m (women)	1000m (men) 800m (women)	javelin (women) / pole vault (men)			
100m	400m	1500m	javelin	pole vault	discus

Going for gold

People have competed in track and field events for thousands of years. The earliest track and field competition took place at the first Olympic Games in ancient Greece. The only event was a sprint from one end of the stadium to the other!

The 100-meter race is one of the most popular events at the Summer Olympics.

Track today

Today, track and field competitions take place in countries around the world. The Olympic Games, the World Championships in Athletics, and the Pan American Games are some of the biggest and most important track and field competitions. There are also many national and local track and field events.

The International Association of Athletics Federations (IAAF) organizes many worldwide athletics competitions, including the VTB Bank World Athletics Final.

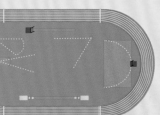

Track stars

Track and field athletes train hard to become the best in their sport. The fastest and strongest men and women become track stars like Jamaica's Usain Bolt. In 2009, Bolt ran the 100-meter race in a record 9.58 seconds! He ruled the 100-meter, 200-meter, and 4x100-meter races at the last two Olympic Games.

Bolt is called the "world's fastest man."

Keeping track

Many years after her death, U.S. runner Florence Griffith-Joyner still holds the record for the women's 100-meter race. Jesse Owens and Carl Lewis are two other celebrated American sprinters in history. Star athletes who are still competing today include Jamaicans Yohan Blake and Shelly-Ann Fraser-Pryce, Americans Allyson Felix and Carmelita Jeter, Kenyan David Rudisha, and British runner Mo Farah.

Allyson Felix is an American sprint athlete who has won gold and silver medals in the 200-meter race as well as three gold medals in women's relay races.

World's greatest athletes

Because an athlete in combined events has to be the best in so many different events, the winner is often called "the world's greatest athlete." U.S. athlete Ashton Eaton won the decathlon at the 2012 Olympic Games in London. American athletes Jim Thorpe and Bruce Jenner have also won the decathlon event in previous Olympic Games.

Ashton Eaton holds the world record for both decathlon and heptathlon.

Heptathlon heroes

British athlete Jessica Ennis powered her way through seven events to win the women's heptathlon at the 2012 Olympics. American athlete Jackie Joyner-Kersee did the same more than 20 years ago.

Jackie Joyner-Kersee's record in the heptathlon still stands today.

Get on track!

You do not have to be a track star to take part in track and field events. You could join a track and field club in your area to practice and compete in track meets. A track meet is a competition between different teams, schools, or clubs. Most track meets last for a day and include a number of different events. Most schools also hold track meets each year.

These girls are competing in a 60-meter race at a track meet held by the Kamloops Track and Field Club in Kamloops, Canada.

Choose your sport

With so many track and field events, there is something for everyone! Different events test the speed, strength, or stamina of competitors. Choose the events that are right for you. Then lace up your running shoes, get on track, and have a field day!

A high school team in Florida stretches before a track and field meet.

Glossary

Note: Boldfaced words that are defined in the text may not appear in the glossary.

clear Jump over an object without touching it

competitor A person who takes part in a track and field event

disqualified No longer allowed to compete in an event

eliminated Knocked out of the competition

foul line A marked line a competitor is not allowed to cross

lane A narrow section of a race track

lead leg The first leg a runner lifts over a hurdle

leg One section of a relay race

relay A race in which teammates take turns running

sprint A short race; also to run very fast

stadium A large sports arena with seats for people to watch events

staggered Starting lines that are spaced evenly so the inner lanes of a track are not shorter

stamina The ability to do a hard or tiring activity for a long time

starting block An object on a track that a runner pushes off from at the start of a race

torso The trunk or main part of a body without the arms, legs, or head

trail leg The second leg a runner lifts over a hurdle

Index